TEENAGE
REBELLION

TEENAGE REBELLION

WILLIAM LEE CARTER, Ed.D.

Rapha Publishing/Word, Inc.

Houston and Dallas, TX

Teenage Rebellion
by William Lee Carter, Ed.D. Copyright ©
Rapha Publishing/Word, Inc., 1991,
Houston and Dallas, TX.

First Printing, 1991
ISBN: 0-945276-35-4
Printed in the United States of America

CONTENTS

THE REBELLIOUS YEARS

Ask most parents to describe the behavior of a teenager and you will be told that some form of rebellion takes place during these years. In fact, many parents feel that the adolescent years consist of one act of rebellion after another. Some of the more common expressions of teenagers' rebellious behavior patterns include:

- Breaking promises to follow a prescribed code of conduct established by the parent

- Claiming ignorance of parental expectation, even though both parent and teen know the teenager is being deceitful

- Challenging beliefs that have governed the family's behavior for years

- Deliberately flaunting inappropriate behavior as a way of exercising control over a disagreeing parent

- Rejecting standards set by adults, thinking them to be outdated for today's youth

- Forcing adults to agree to change by overstating the need for a new set of guidelines

Of all the teenagers I see in my counseling practice, those I enjoy most have frequently been described by their parents as rebellious. Once the rebellious teenagers have become convinced of my interest in their points of

2

view, they frequently spill their hearts out, hoping I will understand them. They often respond to my listening with a sense of emotional relief.

My characteristic way of approaching behavioral problems of youth is to consider matters from the teenager's point of view. Although I am not likely to agree with the teen in all areas of concern, my knowledge of his or her viewpoint provides invaluable information that I can eventually use in providing a beneficial response.

UNDERSTANDING TEENAGE REBELLION

Rebellion Is Necessary for Adolescent Development

You can imagine the reactions I receive from parents when I tell them a teenager needs to experience rebellious feelings in order to fully develop into responsible adults. Some parents interpret my statement as approval of adolescent anarchy. Others recognize the truth of my words but dread facing their reality.

Of course, I am not advocating that all rebellion is desirable, nor am I proposing that parents learn to enjoy their teenagers' acts of insubordination. However, full comprehension of the adolescents' reaction to their world allows the parent to be more objective in selecting a productive course of action for the family. Through rebellion, the teenagers may be:

- Actively questioning the value of the limits their parents have placed around their behavior

- Searching for answers to their questions about their families' beliefs

- Moving toward their eventual need to be independent of their families

- Testing others to determine if they can be counted on for guidance through life's difficult times

- Trying out their own problem-solving skills to judge how capable they really are

- Making a statement of their need to control their own little corner of the world

I believe the overwhelming concern of most parents is that their teenagers' rebellious behavior will include mistakes that will result in long-lasting emotional scars. The strong reaction of the parent to the rebellious adolescent typically represents the parent's statement of concern for the young person. Through his or her reaction, the parent is saying, *I love you too much to let you make a wreck of your life.* The inexperienced youth, though, commonly misunderstands the parent's concern and counters with behavior that suggests, *If you really love me, you will let me do as I please. Trust me. I know what I'm doing.*

In time, the teenagers will realize the folly of their rebellion. But until that day, parents must properly balance restraint and permissiveness. A common question of the parents, then, is, "If our teenagers must experience rebellion, how far do we allow them to fall before we reach down to pick them up?"

I recall one teenage girl, Jamie, who made the mistake of associating with a peer group that could only be described as "trouble." The values of Jamie's new circle of friends contrasted sharply with the Christian values her family depended on for guidance.

Jamie's rebellious stance posed a dilemma for the family. Recognizing Jamie's need to come to her own conclusions about the social values she would eventually embrace, her mom and dad wanted to avoid being overly protective. But they simultaneously feared that permissiveness could result in monumental errors in judgment by their daughter.

Responding appropriately to such rebellion requires a closer look at the dynamics of teenage rebellion and its role in adolescent growth. The following case study will illustrate some of these dynamics.

Adolescent Mistakes Lead to Personal Growth

Victor and I had known one another for quite a few years. I first became acquainted with him when he was a 14-year-old ninth-grader struggling to make passing grades in school. He came from a family that was strongly dependent on Christian values. His parents were well thought of by their peers and had positions of leadership in their church and community.

Victor struggled through his adolescent years, moving from one rebellious stance to another. He deliberately did poorly in school, claiming the classes were useless to him. He dabbled in alcohol abuse periodically and seemed to delight in coming home in a drunken stupor occasionally just to prove to his parents that he was bold enough to violate their standards of conduct. He reached a point in his adolescence when he announced his freedom from his religious training and declared that he was not sure God even existed. The clashes Victor had with his parents were frequent during those teenage years.

He entered early adulthood with feelings of contempt for his parents. Once he was living on his own, however, he discovered that his steadfast, rebellious views on life were not as valid as he had once thought them to be. At the age of 22, Victor was willing to reexamine the teachings he had been given by his parents from an early age. Financially broke, educationally untrained, spiritually empty, and deemed irresponsible by his friends, Victor was ready to learn from his mistakes.

I told Victor one of my favorite biblical characters is the Prodigal Son, the epitome of a rebellious youth. This parable is enacted daily in our modern society as adolescents make mistakes in their lives, only to later learn that their parents were not quite as archaic in their thinking as they had previously assumed.

The depths to which teenagers must go to learn from their rebellion depends on several variables, which include:

• The inborn disposition of the young person

• Adult responses of understanding, or lack of it, offered to the child during his or her years of character development

• Stress or trauma in the family that is beyond the control of either the teen or the parents

• Influences of the culture or environment in which the young person is reared

• The presence or absence of healthy role models in the teen's life

• The degree to which parents notice early signs of rebellion and take quick preventative action

- Successes the child has had in coercing the parents to give him or her control of decision-making powers at an early age

To return to Victor's case study, he and I had numerous talks about the origins of his rebellion and the lessons he had learned from his mistakes. Among the insights he shared was his belief that his parents had been too quick to satisfy his whims and desires as a young boy. In a conference with Victor and his parents, his mom explained, "We thought we were doing the right thing when you were young by providing you with all the pleasures we could reasonably afford. We thought you would appreciate it more than you did."

"But Mom," asked a genuinely interested son, "why did you think I would automatically be grateful to you and Dad? Didn't you think for a moment that you were spoiling me and setting me up for a rebellious adolescence?"

Knowing she could talk frankly with her adult son and be more fully understood, Mom confided, "Victor, at the time, we didn't recognize our error. I think if we had been more honest with ourselves about your strong temperament we probably would have given you less. But another factor was the pressure we felt from our own peer group. Most of our friends provided well for their children and we didn't want you to have any less."

Examination of Victor's case pinpoints several factors that contributed to his rebellion. His personality style was such that he was prone to confrontation with authority figures. Trying to soothe their son's irritability, his parents went beyond the extra mile to please him. Victor pointed out to his mother that perhaps they had been too quick to satisfy his demands. Despite the factors influencing Victor's rebellion, he was able to extract valuable bits of wisdom from his experiences.

Not all adolescents endure the same degree of harm from their rebellious actions. Some adolescents pass into adulthood with few adjustment problems, while others are an emotional wreck throughout the teen years and well into adult life. The lessons a young person learns through rebellion may depend on the traumatic impact of the teen's errors and the wisdom of his or her parents as they try to provide guidance to the struggling youth.

Rebellion Highlights the Teen's Need for Control

I believe one of the most important words parents need to understand in effectively influencing their teenager is the word *control*. In some form or fashion we all want to be in control of our lives. At times it is difficult to recognize ways in which both adults and children employ control measures. We typically think of control involving an aggressive act in which one person attempts to dominate another. Certainly, aggression can represent control, but so can other forms of behavior. Parental control plays an important role in shaping the life of a young person. These controlling efforts may be positive or negative. For example:

- A 17-year-old is required to pay for his first car so he will appreciate its value.

- A high-school senior is given a specific price range for selecting a dress for her prom.

- Angry at her daughter for violating a rule, a mother screams threats of punishment at the girl.

- Disgusted at his son's poor report card, a father refuses to talk to the son as evidence of his displeasure.

- A daughter is promised a much-desired violin if only she will maintain a B average in school.

As you can see by the above examples, a parent's efforts to control the teenager may be either good or bad, depending on the motivation behind the control tactic. Because adolescents need controls, it is healthy and desirable to give guidelines and reasonable boundaries for them. Yet parents' efforts to control through threats, coercion, the silent treatment, or similar tactics can give teens a message of mistrust. The stage can be set for the teenagers to retaliate with controlling reactions of their own. For example:

- Feeling ignored by his father, whose attention and approval he so desperately desires, a 15-year-old boy resorts to petty thievery. He hopes to simultaneously gain his dad's attention and punish him for his inactive parenting.

- A teenage girl shouts at her mother, accusing her of being more interested in her job than her family.

- Afraid of her father's stern nature, a 13-year-old girl sits stone-faced as her angry dad attempts to get her to explain about her inappropriate behavior with a boy. She fears her father will ridicule her.

- Not wanting to be grounded for a failing grade, a ninth-grade boy signs his dad's name to a progress report sent home by his teacher. He plans to raise his average before report cards are issued.

Ideally, young persons should be offered increased opportunities to be in control of their lives as they grow older. There are times, however, that teenagers mistakenly assume they are ready for more responsibility than they can effectively manage. In other instances parents may hold on to controls too long, leaving the teenagers feeling strangled in their hope for increased freedom. Either of these two family situations can leave the door open for a power struggle from which neither the parents nor the teenagers emerge satisfied. Contrast the way in which two teenagers attempt to control their parents in these two examples:

Mark, age 14, was actively involved in athletics, school, and church activities. His commitment to these obligations was so strong he neglected even the simplest of duties required of him at home. He responded to his mother's reasonable requests by making excuses, whining, and throwing emotional tantrums. Not wanting to touch off a major war with their son, Mark's parents tried to be as understanding as possible. In response to their flexibility, Mark simply grew increasingly rebellious.

Eighteen-year-old Melissa had been known throughout her childhood and adolescence as pleasant and cooperative. When, as a high-school senior, she rebelled against her parents, shock waves rumbled through her circle of friends. No longer willing to comply with her parents' strict rules on dating, curfew, and spending, Melissa wrestled control from her parents by uncharacteristically breaking rules, arguing her point, and accusing her parents of mistrust.

While Mark's case typifies a teenager who rebels out of his unwillingness to view life from any perspective except his own, Melissa's example demonstrates how an otherwise compliant teenager can become rebellious when she feels overpowered by doubting parents. Like Mark, Melissa engaged her parents in struggles for control, hoping her exaggerated emotional expressions would bring understanding to her domineering parents.

Understanding teenage rebellion is much easier when parents remember that we all have a need to be in control. Certainly parents, with their God-given position of family leadership, must maintain ultimate responsibility. Exercising healthy control over teenagers is vital. So, too, is it necessary to recognize the needs of teenagers and their increasing urge to assume control of their lives. This issue will be discussed in more detail later in this booklet.

Rebellion Is a Communication Device

I had an experience several years ago while teaching a Sunday school class of high-school students that provided a useful insight into one of the driving forces behind teenage rebellion. Our focus that day centered around the change that occurs when someone replaces his or her old, destructive nature with a renewed knowledge of Christian principles that govern behavior.

One of the teenagers in the class read Colossians 3:8, which states "But now you also, put them all aside: anger, wrath, malice, slander, and abusive speech from your mouth." As soon as these words had been read, another teenage boy, who had a reputation for rebellion, blurted out, "If I quit doing all those things, I'd never get anything across to anybody. No one takes me seriously if I don't force my feelings on them!"

This young man lived in a world that lacked the open kind of communication that would allow him to tell others his innermost thoughts and emotions without receiving a negative backlash. Unable to freely express himself, he resorted to angry outbursts, hateful statements, and cursing in the desperate hope that someone would accurately interpret the hurt he felt within.

This rebellious young man was saying that before he could "put on a heart of compassion, kindness, humility, gentleness and patience" (Colossians 3:12), others would have to convey their understanding of his point of view. Until that message was given to him, he would continue to risk rebellion as an outgrowth of his communication failure.

One of the basic tenets of understanding the communication between any two individuals is that words, alone, do not sufficiently convey what is being communicated. To fully understand the intent of the message, we must also consider:

• The tone of voice being used

• The emotional intensity of the voice

• The context in which the message is being rendered

• The body gestures of the speaker

• The rate of speech being used

• The background and knowledge of the speaker

Certainly the list could continue. As we find ourselves in conversations with adolescents, too often we fail to take into full account all the factors that go into the teenagers' efforts to communicate. It becomes easy to focus on only a portion of these factors, to the exclusion of others.

At a workshop I conducted for parents, the participants and I generated a list of parents' thoughts and emotions that stand in the way of effective communication with teenagers. Some of the more enlightening reactions included:

- "My child has no right to think that about me or anyone else."

- "If I let him get away with that statement, he'll think he can run right over me."

- "When I was her age, I wouldn't have dreamed of talking as she does."

- "These teenagers don't know half as much as they think they know."

- "He always overreacts to the most trivial things."

- "If only I could reason with him, he would see the logic of my point of view."

- "If I admit she's right, I'll never hear the end of it."

- "I need to put a stop to this right now before it gets any worse."

Most teenagers learn quickly that negative emotional expressions are not accepted by most adults. Yet being unskilled in the subtle art of communicating with others, most teenagers know of no other way to make their desired point than to turn up the volume until rebellion results.

One teenage girl, Jodi, traced the roots of her rebellion for me. Recalling her father's persistent failure to give her attention, Jodi told me, "I *felt* rebellious for a long time before I *acted* rebellious." Losing the hope that her dad would change his ways and notice her, Jodi rebelled through school failure, alcohol abuse, sexual promiscuity, and disruption of the home. At the root of her behavior was a desperate hope of communicating her need for fatherly love.

Lest I tacitly imply that rebellious communication *solely* takes only the form of obvious acts of defiance, I should point out that rebellion can be of a passive nature as well. Many teenagers use passive forms of communicating rebellion. They may choose this strategy because silent rebellion cannot be as readily challenged, but it can be used as a way of expressing displeasure. Some of the ways a teenager can passively rebel, and the unspoken messages of these behaviors, include:

• Refusal to talk to others (*If you don't know what I'm thinking, you can't criticize me.*)

• Failure to achieve (*You apparently think I'm incompetent, so I'll give you proof you are correct.*)

- Daydreaming (*If I can't feel important in the real world, I'll make my own world in which I am important.*)

- Acting helpless (*You tell me I can't do anything on my own, so I'll let someone do it for me.*)

- Concealing information (*There's no way I will reveal the truth. If I did I would be open for criticism or punishment.*)

- Claiming ignorance (*I'll prove I'm the uninformed person people think I am.*)

- Giving a half-hearted effort (*I'll do what I have to do, but I refuse to do it to your satisfaction.*)

- Lack of motivation (*I've lost faith in myself in the same way that others have lost faith in me.*)

Because rebellion is a risky form of communication, teens seldom experience success in building relationships through this method of behavior. Yet they continue to gamble in the hope that relief will be given to them in the form of understanding.

THE EMOTIONS OF THE REBELLIOUS TEENAGER

As previously noted, rebellion is often a communication form used by teenagers. Granted, this style of communicating is sometimes crude in nature, but it is their attempt to let others know their feelings. However, prolonged rebellion during adolescence can result in emotional harm. This section will explore three common emotional conditions that often occur in rebellious teenagers: depression, guilt, and anxiety.

Depression and Rebellion

It is hard for many parents and other adults to recognize the depression that often accompanies teenage rebellion. The typical haughty, arrogant attitude of most rebellious teenagers suggests anything but depression. However, one of the ground rules of human behavior is that the overexpression of emotions often is a strong indicator of more serious, underlying emotional discomfort. This is the case in the rebellious teenager.

Dissatisfaction is frequently substituted as a synonym for the term *depression.* Rebellious teenagers are frequently dissatisfied with various aspects of their lives. One teenage girl said, "I can't tell you how many things are wrong in my life. I can't get along with my parents. I'm constantly in trouble at home. At school, my teachers act like I'm some sort of snob. They treat me like a juvenile delinquent. The only teenagers who will have anything to do with me are the ones who are always in trouble, just like me.

I know I'm going nowhere in life, but I don't know how to stop. In fact, I'm not sure I *want* to stop."

This teenage girl's rebellion was an expression of the despair that had engulfed her. Other people characterized her as self-centered, conceited, arrogant, and difficult to manage—and she certainly showed those traits. But the term that described her real feelings was not *arrogant*, but depressed. She had become convinced that life had little to offer her. Her rebellion was an expression of the hopeless circumstances surrounding her.

Guilt

Franklin never would have admitted to his parents what he told me. As he and I discussed his offensive behavioral characteristics, he confessed, "You know my dad isn't doing too well physically. He has high blood pressure and he's under a lot of stress. His doctor has told him that if his life doesn't become less stressful, he's a high risk for a heart attack." As Franklin thought about what he had just said, he added with a chuckle, "You know, I'm a big part of the stress in his life." Next, he began to think of the emotions that might overwhelm him if his father *did* experience a heart attack. In a rare, thoughtful moment, he expressed, "I'd feel pretty bad if my dad had a heart attack and I knew it was partly my fault." He sat silently for a moment and then shrugged off his emotions. "Oh well, I can't worry about that. I don't want to get too soft. If I do, my parents will think they've won." He smiled at me as he spoke these words, but we both knew he was feeling guilty about his rebellious behavior.

Remorse is a positive and constructive emotion; it causes the discomfort that can motivate the young person to make positive changes. Guilt, however, is condemning and destructive. Christ's death paid for our sin, guilt, and condemnation. The Holy Spirit's conviction of our sinful behavior is not motivated out of His desire to condemn and punish us, but to constructively discipline, shape, and help us. Rebellious teenagers, like Franklin, may run from feelings of guilt because giving in to them may mean having to honestly confront the negative effects of their argumentative ways.

Franklin's admission of guilty feelings marked a turning point in his behavior. As if he had let the cat out of the bag, he could no longer feel comfortable displaying the rebellious behavior that had become his trademark. His guilt caused him to feel sufficiently disgusted with himself so that he became open to the guidance of adults who were willing to teach him more effective relationship skills.

Anxiety and Fear

Whether or not rebellious teenagers will acknowledge it, they are fearful of many things. Like Franklin, they may fear the eventual results of their rebellious actions.

Many rebellious teenagers also fear they will never outgrow their argumentative ways and will find themselves in perennial hot water with others.

Some teenagers fear they will never be understood and will be doomed to relationships marred by conflict. I heard two teenagers talking about this particular fear. One said to the other, "If my family is an example of what family life is all about, there's no way I'll ever get married and have children."

In many rebellious teenagers I find a sensitivity that is hidden from others. This sensitivity causes them to want to be accepted as a person of worth and value. They want to know they "belong" to both their family and their peer groups. The force of rebellious behavior invariably causes a loss in these relationships. This loss creates an uncomfortable feeling in the teenager. This discomfort may be shown in a variety of ways.

For example, anxiety may be shown as follows:

- Frequent complaints of physical illness, including headaches, stomachaches, and sleep disturbances
- Feelings of panic that result in unbridled emotional expression
- Unrealistic preoccupations or irrational beliefs about others
- Intense emotional displays that go beyond what the situation calls for
- Becoming numb to the emotions of others for fear of further emotional hurt
- Assuming that the worst will always happen
- Holding emotions within to the point that bodily tension becomes uncomfortable

These three emotions—depression, guilt, and anxiety—are frequent characteristics of a rebellious teenager. Recurring argumentativeness between a teenager and his or her family members can take its toll on the young person's emotional condition, resulting in distorted displays of these and other emotions that bring chronic displeasure to both the teen and his or her parents.

PARENTAL RESPONSES TO TEENAGE REBELLION

To be confronted by a teenager who is emotionally dishonest is certainly not a comfortable feeling. It can even be an offensive experience. Many parents tell me, "I've tried everything I can think of to stop my teenager from being rebellious. I've grounded him, taken away every privilege he has, removed his favorite items from his room, and even ignored him. And nothing seems to work!"

One of the first steps in successfully dealing with adolescent uprisings is to recognize that teenagers have a need to act as they do and they will not quickly give up in their effort to be fully understood. As difficult as it may be, we must first step outside ourselves and look at the world from the teenage viewpoint in order to correctly select the most useful responses to be offered.

Demonstrate Patience in the Presence of Rebellion

The practical wisdom of the Book of James tells us to "be quick to hear, slow to speak and slow to anger; for the anger of man does not achieve the righteousness of God" (James 1:19–20). These words can become the foundation of a productive communication pattern between parent and child that effectively reduces the teen's need to be rebellious. The problem most of us have in following James's directions is the part about being slow to speak and slow to express our anger. To do so requires a patience that is difficult to cultivate.

One man explained to me the difficulty he has being patient with his two teenage children. "I get frustrated with my own inability to exhibit patience toward my children. To be perfectly honest, I seem to have patience with everyone but my own kids. I have a demanding job with a lot of responsibility, but I can easily maintain my composure at work. When I'm with my friends, I rarely get upset. In fact, my peers usually turn to me for help because they know I'll stay calm in the midst of a storm. At home, though, it's a different story. One of my teenagers does the least little thing and I get upset and fly off the handle. Then I feel guilty and vow never to lose my temper again. Before you know it, though, something will happen and I do the very thing I pledged not to do!"

The relationship between parent and child is, of course, different than any other. As we study our relationships with our children it becomes quickly evident how difficult it is to separate ourselves emotionally from our children. To a large degree, parents live through the lives of their children. This simple dynamic can be seen in each of the following examples:

- Feeling as if his own name were on the school honor roll, a father beams at his son's good school grades.

- Nervous for her daughter as she embarks on her first date, a mom continually thinks of the girl throughout the evening.

- Bothered by his son's public carousing, a father shows great concern for the negative reputation his son is developing.

The evidence of parental investment in teenagers is in the parents' emotional reactions. Invariably, the parent becomes emotionally involved in the child's activities as a byproduct of parental love. It is natural to want what is best for our children.

A wise, older man whose children had grown and left home years earlier told me that he began to be a better parent when he realized he was most effective as a father when he learned to set aside his own emotions so he could accurately interpret the behavior of his children. By foregoing the need to live through his children, he found them more open to the guidance he could offer by virtue of his advanced experience in life.

Returning to James's guidance to "be quick to hear, slow to speak and slow to anger," we realize James is encouraging us to work at correctly perceiving the behavior of others. Thus, in developing patience as a helpful response to a rebellious teenager, we must accurately interpret the message the teenager is sending through his or her rebellious actions. To do so requires the adult to step away from his or her own needs momentarily and into the world of the young person.

As one mother and I discussed this parental challenge, she told me, "I have a hard time thinking like my daughter does, even though when I was her age I thought just like she does now. But as an adult, I can see the disadvantage of her interpretation of the world. I try to teach her out of my own understanding because I don't want her to have to wait until she's an adult to benefit from a more mature view of life."

The very fact that a teenager fails to accept the enlightenment of a more experienced adult tells us the teen must face a certain degree of frustration until he or she has accumulated sufficient experience and wisdom. Accepting this inevitable part of adolescent development positively, the parent, through his or her comprehension of the teenager's world, can be an effective guide to that young person. With patience, the parent can eventually experience that internal joy that results from seeing the teenager grow in wisdom. The behavioral, emotional, and spiritual growth of a rebellious teenager can be positively influenced by the patience of an understanding parent.

Allow Rebellion to Result in Communication

Since parents are naturally willing to display their love for their children, they can often be successful in understanding the teens' points of view. Convincing adolescents that their points of view are understood, however, may be an altogether different matter. Parents may have difficulty knowing how to put into words their accurate perceptions. The adolescents may have built up sufficient negativism toward their families that they can be hard to convince that the parents do, indeed, understand them accurately.

The psalmist poetically writes, "Search me, O God, and know my heart; / Try me and know my anxious thoughts; / And see if there be any hurtful way in me, / And lead me in the everlasting way" (Psalms 139:23–24). Using our heavenly Father's understanding of His children as a model, parents of teenagers must have a primary goal of reflecting their understanding back to their children. Parents who enter the teenagers' world and search with them for solutions to potential problems can be more effective helpers to their children. Several guidelines should be followed in showing your teenager that you understand him or her:

• Concentrate on both the words and gestures of the teenager to fully comprehend his or her present emotional state.

• In your own words, restate what your teen has said to show that you are listening.

• Choose your words carefully so you aren't perceived as being condescending or judgmental.

• Keep your physical posture relaxed so your words and actions match.

• Verbally respond to feelings the teen is not expressing, but is obviously feeling.

• Offer your own opinion or advice only after your teenager has had full opportunity to express himself or herself.

• Keep your comments brief.

It's ironic, but we often are most effective in communicating with others when we refrain from excessive talking. When dealing with rebellious adolescents, it is helpful to allow them to verbalize their emotions with the expectation that they will regain a sense of control on their own. Active listening shows them their opinions are being taken seriously.

Following are examples of how potentially explosive exchanges can be reduced in their emotional intensity through a parent's willingness to listen:

• Thirteen-year-old boy: "I can't stand it! My math teacher says I have to do all this work by tomorrow. Doesn't she understand? I'll never get through with all this homework!"

Father: "You're loaded with work tonight. You're under a lot of pressure from your teacher to get it all done by tomorrow."

• Fourteen-year-old daughter: "Mom, Wendy and I were having a good time until her mood changed. She was so gripey, I just wanted to get away from her."

Mother: "It certainly makes you wonder what caused her sudden mood change."

• Seventeen-year-old son: "Dad, I hate to tell you, but you need to come outside with me and look what just happened to your car."

Father (concerned, but calm): "This doesn't sound like good news to me. I'll bet you weren't thrilled to have to come and tell me. Let's go take a look at it."

• Fifteen-year-old daughter: "I don't want to come home at eleven o'clock. That's too early!"

Father: "It seems unfair when I set your curfew earlier than you'd like."

Trouble is ahead for parents who engage in conversation in which opinions are offered, directions are given, constructive criticism is presented, or consequences are levied before they display a willingness to listen. Failure to demonstrate accurate understanding may encourage a teenager to:

• Throw a verbal tantrum with the intent to manipulate

• Attempt to deceive through distorting the facts

• Refuse to cooperate by becoming silent

• Retaliate by acting even worse than before

- Shift the focus by pointing out other family members' faults

- Rationalize the behavioral choices that have already been made

The parent's willingness to listen to a potentially rebellious young person can defuse the teen's need to further express his or her message through wayward behavior. By avoiding statements that are harmful to the adolescent, the parent puts the teen in a better position to draw appropriate conclusions regarding the available choices.

Keep the Dialogue Flowing

There is little that can destroy a family more than a breakdown in the communication among family members. In many families, parent and child seldom speak to one another unless it's to mumble, "Pass the salt." In these families both the adult and the teenager wait on one another to take the first step in reestablishing open communication. As time passes, it often becomes apparent that neither will initiate a dialogue to restore a relationship that allows the free exchange of thoughts and emotions. Neither parent nor teen will loosen the grip on the hurt or anger that has displaced family harmony.

Scripture tells us how an anger-based spirit of judgment creates a roadblock to productive relationships. Luke quotes Christ as teaching, "Do not judge and you will not be judged; and do not condemn, and you will not be condemned; pardon, and you will be pardoned" (Luke 6:37).

Because of the gap in experience between adults and adolescents, teenagers will fail to exercise adult wisdom as they make choices. It's tempting for parents to recognize the fault of the young persons' decisions and cast judgment on them. Teenagers who feel condemned are not likely to be cooperative with adults, but instead will harbor resentment. This feeling of resentment then leads to rebellious behavior.

Typical parent responses that can become roadblocks to communication with teenagers include:

- Accusations (*You deliberately did that to irritate me!*)

- Predictions (*If you keep that up, you'll never have any friends.*)

- Sarcasm (*You really think you're cute, don't you?*)

- Name-Calling (*Look at you! You're acting just like a 3-year-old child.*)

- Ignoring (*I refuse to even talk to you about that issue.*)

- Threats (*You keep trying my patience and you'll regret the day you decided to do that.*)

- Procrastination (*I can't talk now. Wait until I'm not so busy.*)

- Interrupting (*Now wait just a minute! That's not how I remember it.*)

- Exasperation (*Go ahead and do what you want. I'm tired of trying to talk to you.*)

It is an interesting dynamic of communication that we are often most effective in our influence over teenagers when we avoid certain statements and refrain from saying more than the teen is able to absorb. I rarely find an adolescent who doesn't care whether his or her parents understand their child's thoughts and emotions. However, many teens identify their greatest source of family strife as the family members' inability to effectively communicate.

Instead of placing stumbling blocks in the path of good communication, parents will be more effective by following these guidelines:

- Show your teen, through words and behavior, that you understand his or her viewpoint.

- Keep criticism to a minimum and use it only after you have actively listened.

- Walk away from arguing, but be firm in your decisions.

- Maintain an open mind. Don't insist you are always right.

- Use proper timing when making negative, but necessary, statements.

- Refrain from trying to emotionally overpower your teen. You won't win.

- Give your teenager a voice in the decision-making process.

- Keep your comments brief.

- Allow your teenager to live with consequences of his or her behavior.

- Show a willingness to approach your child rather than waiting for him or her to approach you.

As the parent shows leadership in family communication, the typical teenager watches carefully before determining the atmosphere is safe for disclosure. As time proves to the young person that words and actions will be interpreted with an open mind, he or she will gradually respond with communication that suggests cooperation in place of competition.

Set Limits According to the Teenager's Need

Not all teenagers will favorably respond to parental efforts to demonstrate understanding through active listening. While some youth will react to the empathetic adult by reducing their emotional demands, others will continue to display evasiveness, deceitfulness, confrontation, or defensiveness in the face of parental control and composure. A learned pattern of rebellion can be difficult for the young person to discard.

The wisdom of Proverbs tell us, "The rod and reproof give wisdom, / But a child who gets his own way brings shame to his mother" (Proverbs 29:15). It is the parent's responsibility to discern which lessons of life the teenager has yet to learn so that appropriate intervention may be made.

Viewing the discipline process this way may allow the parent to more objectively respond to the teenager's need for guidance.

I routinely tell rebellious teenagers that my philosophy of discipline calls for the parent to be as flexible as the teenager allows. Most adolescents quickly accept this way of thinking with the hope that their parents will take this guideline as an endorsement of a permissive system of behavior management. In time, however, teenagers recognize that the freedom extended to or withheld from them is directly related to the choices they make. For example:

- A 13-year-old boy who experiments with alcohol at the urging of his friends should not be given as much latitude in selecting his social activities.

- A teen's responsible management of money may positively influence her parents' decision to co-sign a bank note on a used car.

- An unwillingness to follow the speed limit should result in limited unsupervised driving privileges.

- A teen who virtually always does his or her homework should be allowed to decide whether to study before or after she has viewed TV.

- Following a series of incidences involving lying, a parent would want more evidence before accepting statements by the teenager as the truth.

The reaction of the teenager to parental discipline determines the flexibility displayed on his or her behalf. The role of the parent, then, is to objectively interpret the needs of the teenager, apply appropriate measures to correct mistakes, and allow the teen to draw conclusions about the choices he or she has made. One 14-year-old told me, "When my parents started letting me decide how flexible they would be, at first I liked it a lot because we didn't argue as much. Then I got frustrated because I couldn't get my way as easily as I used to. But now I've learned to quit fighting my parents as much because I know that I am in charge of what happens next to me."

A mother and I concluded our counseling session about her relationship with her teenage children with her comment, "I think I've finally caught on to the secret of handling my kids. I used to fight with them constantly, which was my way of rebelling against their adolescence. Now that I've come to understand their behavior and my responsibility to guide them into adulthood, the tension in our home has been released. I'm no longer angry at being the mother of teenagers who sometimes rebel, and they have no reason to be angry at a mother who refuses to accept their need to express themselves openly." Her words expressed her new sense of satisfaction at their learning experience.

Editor's note

At Rapha, we believe that small groups can provide a nurturing and powerful environment to help people deal with real-life problems such as depression, grief, fear, eating disorders, chemical dependency, codependency, and all kinds of other relational and emotional difficulties. The warmth, honesty, and understanding in those groups helps us understand why we feel and act the way we do. And with the encouragement of others, we can take definitive steps toward healing and health for ourselves and our relationships.

Not all groups, however, provide this kind of "greenhouse" for growth. Some only perpetuate the guilt and loneliness by giving quick and superficial solutions to the deep and often complex problems in our lives.

We urge you to find a group of people in your church, or in a church near you, where the members provide acceptance, love, honesty, and encouragement. Rapha has many different books, workbooks, leader's guides, and types of training so that people in these groups can be nurtured in the love and grace of God and focused on sound biblical principles to help them experience healing and growth.

To obtain a free list of the materials we have available, please write to us at:

Rapha, Inc.
8876 Gulf Freeway, Suite 340
Houston, TX 77017

ABOUT THE AUTHOR. . .

Dr. William Lee Carter is a licensed psychologist at Child Psychiatry Associates in Waco, Texas, a nationally certified school psychologist, and a consultant for Rapha, Inc., serving frequently as a speaker at Rapha conferences and seminars. He received his Doctor of Education degree from Baylor University in 1982. His practice involves consulting with school districts and counseling children, adolescents, and their families in both inpatient and outpatient settings. He and his wife, Julie, have three daughters,

Emily, Sarah, and Mary. He is the author of *The Parent–Child Connection*, *Family Communication*, and *Look Inside Your Child*.